Never Alone

To Meona
May the Lord
bless you
from
Emma -

Never Alone

The True Story of Emma Wawa

Johnny Clark

Published by Johnny & Nicole Clark

ISBN: 978-0-615-46173-1

Printed in the United States of America

DEDICATION

The Wawa Family

Victorien, Emma, Sephora, Eleazar, and Deborah

ACKNOWLEDGEMENTS

To Nicole, my beautiful and patient wife, your inspiration, consistency, and diligence kept this project moving in a forward direction at all times. To Robert Mims, for developing the structure and skilled layout that this book possesses and also for your professional insight and friendship. To Kim Sprecker, your editing skills and well-rounded suggestions made this book truly shine. To John and Julie Clark, my parents, for your unending encouragement, and to my petite mama, Emma Wawa, for believing and trusting in me to tell your amazing story.

Additional contributors include: David Hardiman, Sarah Combs, Emily Cox, and Christina Harris.

It's only because of God, and these amazing people, that this book exists.

Table of Contents

1. A Detour into Darkness – p.11

2. In the Belly of the Beast – p.21

3. Behind Bars: State of Mind, State of Grace – p.27

4. Family Ties: From Africa to America – p.37

5. Out of the Frying Pan, Into the Fire – p.45

6. Imprisoned with Purpose – p.55

7. A Ticket to Ride -- on a Spiritual Roller Coaster – p.75

8. A Spiritual War: Attack and Counterattack – p.87

9. A Celebration of Faith, the Promise of Freedom – p.105

10. An Uncertain Future – p.115

11. An Exit and an Exhortation – p.127

12. 'Betterness' -- not Bitterness – p.139

Chapter One

A Detour into Darkness

"Bonjour! Comment allez-vous?" asks one woman, taking the hand of another. *"Merci. La vie est dure, mais Dieu est Bon. Et vous?"* she replies.

Watching the scene with a smile and slow nod is Emma Wawa. Yes, she thinks, it *is* a good day. And yes, it is true that *"life is hard"* but it is also wonderfully true that *"God is good."*

It would be a mistake to let her small stature fool you. As a nurse's assistant, wife and mother of three children, people know her as a *daughter of heaven*. From the French-speaking nation of Ivory Coast in Africa came Emma Wawa, a figure of irrepressible faith and of solid devotion to God and her family.

Today, Emma is going to testify to God's love and faithfulness before a congregation gathered in Madison,

Wisconsin. Many who hear her story know from her experience that Emma has the ability to speak life into any situation. Her message of love, hope, and encouragement has the ability to penetrate through her listeners' defenses and directly into their souls. Her words carry the power of someone who, when speaking about life, has been with God. Her faith has been significantly tried through a crucible of circumstances that would have left a weak, superficial, self-reliant Christian in a heap of wreckage.

Anyone who has the opportunity to sit with this woman quickly understands the level of authority she carries. It isn't long before she says something like, *"It is the Lord who wants me here today, and there is something that He has put upon my heart to share with you."*

She frequently pauses to look up, smiling as if receiving an unseen caress. When she returns her gaze to her listener, her face shines with peace, confidence, and a tenderness born of pain and loss.

Emma can recite the 91st Psalm with ease. *"Celui qui demeure sous l'abri du Très-Haut Repose à l'ombre du Tout Puissant,"* and in English: *"He who dwells in the shelter of the Most High will rest in the shadow of the Almighty.*"

Emma goes on, her voice growing more fervent with each verse, *"I will say of the LORD, He is my refuge and my fortress, my God, in whom I trust. Surely He will save you from the fowler's snare and from the deadly pestilence. He will cover you with his feathers, and under his wings you will find refuge; his faithfulness will be your shield and rampart. You will not fear the terror of night, nor the arrow that flies by day, nor the pestilence that stalks in the darkness, nor the plague that destroys at midday.*"

As a nurse's assistant, it had started out like any other busy work day at the hospital. During her long shifts Emma had earned the reputation of being a hard-working woman who often found comfort in singing French hymns and could always produce a brilliant smile no matter the task.

This particular day had been especially grueling. Emma's body ached from hours of making beds, cleaning rooms, and helping post-operative patients take their doctor-ordered walks around the nurses' station. So when that night in September 2006 finally came to an end, Emma felt exhasted.

She had no idea that as she clocked out at 11 p.m., she was about to enter a personal twilight zone.

As Emma made her way through the hospital's dark parking garage, she reached for her phone and dialed Victorien, her husband. Calling him after a long day at work often gave her just enough strength to make it home. She felt comforted and protected during those minutes and looked forward to hearing his voice.

"I'm just getting to my car now and will be home shortly," Emma said, her voice sounding nearly as exhausted as she felt. Victorien heard both the spoken and unspoken messages clearly.

"All right, Sweetie. I'll be waiting when you get here. Is there anything special I can have ready for you?" he asked.

"Oh! My back is sore from working today," Emma replied. *"How about a hot bath?"*

"One hot bath, coming right up!" Victorien said, and Emma, despite her bone-deep fatigue, had to smile. *"You are a good husband. See you soon."*

Even when it was late, as it was tonight, Victorien would greet Emma with a smile and listen as she spoke. He would make dinner and prepare a plate for her when she arrived.

After a nice meal, hot bath, and maybe a massage from Victorien's strong hands, there would be bed and precious sleep. *Soon*, Emma thought. *Just stay awake until then*, she admonished herself.

Moments after exiting the parking garage Emma saw the flashing lights of a police car in her rear a view mirror. *What now?* she thought as she dutifully pulled the van over to the side of the road. Emma rolled down her window as the officer approached.

"Hello, officer," she said, trying her best to be polite. *Now was not the time to aggravate the police*, she reminded herself. However, that would prove a commitment extremely difficult to keep before the night was over.

"Hello, Ma'am," the officer said. *"Where are you coming from tonight?"*

Emma was a bit nervous as she answered the officer. *"Well, I'm on my way home from work at the hospital . . . . Am I in trouble?"* Emma asked calmly.

"You were swerving a bit and going over the line," he said, then pointedly asked: *"You haven't been drinking tonight, have you?"*

"Oh, no." Emma tried to explain, *"Perhaps it is because I'm short and the van itself isn't in great shape. Maybe that's why the vehicle was drifting."* She apologized, and to her relief, the officer seemed to believe her – acting like he was ready to cut her some slack.

"OK, Ma'am. Well, since you haven't been drinking I'm not going to ticket you tonight – but I do need to see your driver's license." Emma gladly handed it to him. No ticket! Thank you, she thought. Soon, I'll be home.

Home. Where Victorien waited with a loving embrace and a kiss. *Home.* Where her three children were asleep, peacefully, in their beds. *Home.* Where a thoughtful dinner had been prepared.

The officer came back to the van with a sober look on his face and asked for her Social Security card.

"Why is this taking so long officer? Is there a problem?" Emma asked, digging for the card from inside her purse and then handing it to the officer.

"It looks like you've got issues with Immigration," he said, his tone now decidedly suspicious. *"There's an alert on your file that says you're running and that you don't have a legit address."*

What? Emma thought, her mind racing. *How can I possibly be running?*

With a bit of anxiety growing, Emma began to explain,*"I have lived and worked in Madison for nearly ten years. My husband and I get mail from Immigration at our house all of the time. Maybe there is a mistake with our address."*

"This seems like more of an issue than an address change," the officer stated.

"See", she said, pointing to the address on her driver's license, *"that address is where we have lived for this entire year without problems."*

"Well, uh, I don't know Ma'am," he shrugged. "That's what INS is saying, and I'm afraid I'm going to have to take you downtown tonight."

Several more police cars arrived. Suddenly, Emma's mind was clouded with fear, recalling all of the people that she personally knew who had been deported because of problems with the Immigration and Naturalization Service.

Don't panic, Emma told herself as she looked up to see the small army of police officers headed toward her van.

"Put your hands where I can see them, and step out of the car slowly," one officer commanded.

With hands hovering over their holstered handguns, several officers slowly approached the van as Emma got out. They muttered accusations about her being an illegal alien as they handcuffed her.

"We have a federal warrant from the U.S. Immigration Department," they said. "It appears you haven't responded to them in six years!"

As she was being pushed into the police car, Emma pleaded for the chance to call home. The cop snapped in reply, *"Are you LISTENING to me? I said, 'NO'! Comprende?"*

The officer who had originally pulled her over, intervened, *"Let her call home, she's cooperated and done everything we've asked. She's got family! She can use my phone."*

The two officers continued to argue, and Emma eventually got to call. *"Make it quick,"* she was told, the squad car door closed and she had her chance.

"Immigration? Oh, no!" a stunned Victorien blurted out as Emma quickly explained. Then regaining his composure, he added, *"I'm coming down there right now to work this out. I'm not going to let them take you. This is just a filing mistake with our new address or something!"*

"No! Don't come – they could arrest you too. Please don't, Victorien; the children need you, and we can't leave them alone," Emma pleaded.

An instantly overwhelmed and helpless Victorien began to panic. Dropping to his knees he told her, *"I'm sorry, Emma. I'm so sorry. . . . just cooperate with them and call me as soon as you can."*

The officer opened the door and indicated that her time was up. With handcuffs engaged, she willingly surrendered the phone to the officer with Victorien still listening on the other end. The officer ended the call and walked away. Emma sat alone watching as a group of officers tore through her van as if they expected to find something terrible. Eventually, the raid ended, and the squad car containing Emma drove to police headquarters.

Chapter Two

In the Belly of the Beast

"We must be confident of our position in the Lord if we are to rise above and conquer all fear," Emma declares. *"Ah, you say, but if only we KNEW God, then we could trust Him."* Quickly and with stern correction, *"No! We MUST know upon whom we stand. Dwelling comes before resting, and if you do not belong to the Lord, then he cannot protect you. Protection is the assurance we have from our Father!"*

Thumbing through the pages of her worn Bible, she begins to read from Matthew 23: *"O Jerusalem, how often I have longed to gather your children together, as a hen gathers her chicks under her wings, but you were not willing."*

Emma smiles, *"You know how a hen gathers her chicks and spreads her wings around them? She doesn't want a vulture to see even one. The love that hen has for her young can be compared to that of the Father's love for us. That's why He speaks of dwelling in the 'shadow of the Almighty.'"*

Being arrested for the first time in her life was an ordeal of confusion, intimidation and fear. There is no comfort to be had when considered a criminal.

Despite her insistence that she had not been drinking that night, an officer escorted her into a small room for a Breathalyzer test. His disdain for this African immigrant woman was obvious by his loud, slow tone reserved for someone he assumed could not speak English.

"This . . . is . . . a . . . BREATHALYZER," the cop sounded out the words. *"Blow into this so we can find out how much you've been drinking."*

When Emma seemed to hesitate, he pointed at the device's mouthpiece. *"Just . . . put . . . your . . . mouth . . . here . . . and . . . blow,"* he seemed to holler.

Emma swallowed her growing frustration, put her lips on the mouthpiece, and blew as ordered. When the officer checked the readout, it showed no alcohol content. *Zero.* He threw the device to the table and led Emma to a holding cell already occupied by a woman, unconscious on the floor.

"You're going to have wait here while we process your file," the officer said, as Emma entered the cell.

"In HERE?" Emma asked, both afraid and confused. The small space reeked of stale sweat, soiled clothing and vomit. With an avid appreciation for cleanliness, she struggled to keep her head from spinning and her stomach from rolling.

"Yep," the jailer said with a grin.

Composing herself, Emma forced politeness into her voice. *"Sir, could I please rinse my mouth? That machine left a bad taste."* He responded with an annoyed *"Psshhh!"* There would be no rinse. The door shut with a clang.

"Wait! Sir, what is going to happen to me?" Emma pleaded.

"Well, they'll either let you go, or they'll send you to Dodge County. That's a maximum security prison, and if you go there it will be for at least ninety days, unless they deport you sooner," he smirked.

As the jailer walked away, whistling an unrecognizable tune, Emma looked at the concrete floor and stared at the unconscious woman.

She buried her head in her hands and whispered, *"What is going on here? I do not deserve this!"*

By now, at the Wawa home the bathtub had spilled over and soaked the floor: dinner was cold. It was now past 1 a.m. The children were awake listening as their father desperately petitioned heaven on his wife's behalf.

Victorien, being the father he was, gathered his children Sephora, age 12; Eleazer, age 11; and Deborah, age 8. He explained what had happened to their mother. He tried his best to withhold any uncertainty or fear and suggested that they trust in the Lord.

After comforting and assuring the children, he went to the phone and called the immigration lawyer they had been working with since arriving in the United States in 1992.

It had been months since the lawyer had returned any calls, and Victorien was reluctant to try this time. But he was desperate.

After many rings, the answering machine finally picked up. Victorien began, *"Hello, this is Victorien Wawa. We have a big problem! My wife has been arrested and taken into custody because of immigration alert on her file. I don't understand why there would any alerts stating that we're not cooperating with INS. Please call me back as soon as possible."*

Desperately waiting, he tried again, *"You assured me that we were in the clear. Why haven't you returned any of my phone messages these past few months? After the tens of thousands of dollars we've paid you, the LEAST you could do is call me back! Please! My wife is in trouble and we need your help. Call me!"* he concluded, sighing as he returned the phone to its cradle.

The children sat together, huddled on the couch, and listened as their father continued to make desperate calls. Victorien never left the kitchen that night, lost in a sea of questions.

Chapter Three

Behind Bars: State of Mind, State of Grace

Emma takes a deep breath before continuing. *"If I were to give up every time I didn't understand why something was happening, I wouldn't be here today, and you wouldn't be listening to my story. When our mind fails to comprehend life's challenging situations, our spirit must lead us. You will find direction and purpose when you're close to the Lord. His promised provision and protection will go before you in everything, every time, no matter the outcome."*

Emma explains why Psalm 91 is so dear to her. *"Fear will come, that's life. It is after we hand that fear to the Father that we can expect mountains to move. Then, during the storm, we can find rest, because we are in the shadow of the Almighty,"* she declares.

Her face was stained with tears and etched with worry. Any hope that Emma had of being released was soon crushed after a guard opened the holding cell door and unceremoniously escorted her to an elevator that led further into the bowels of the Dane County Jail.

When the elevator lurched to a stop and its doors opened, she was led into a bigger cell equipped with two bunk beds. The guard pointed to an empty mattress. Two inmates were watching with cold curiosity and smirked: *"Don't touch my s***."* The guard left.

Sitting on a the thin, stained mattress, lost in worry, Emma wanted nothing more than to curl into a tight little ball, fall asleep, and awake from this nightmare. Instead, her misery was interrupted by a voice.

"If you even think about starting some s***, I'll f*** you up, nig***," one of the women warned.

Emma, laying cold with fear, quietly asked, *Why am I in here with these horrible people?*

As she waited for a blow to the back of the head or a shank to the spine, a second voice asked, *"Why are YOU here?"*

In a mode of defense, Emma snapped, *"Why do you want to know?"*

"Don't get fresh with me, girl. I only asked a simple question," the inmate responded.

"I don't know why I'm here," Emma said, hoping they would leave her alone, *"I don't know."*

But this jailhouse tag team was not about to be denied. *"Well, why did they put you in here?"*

They were not letting up, Emma realized. So she gave in and told them, *"Immigration problems, I guess."*

The answer brought an obnoxious laugh from the first woman. *"Oh! So they wanna send yo' a** back to Africa, huh?"* Hilarious. Or so it seemed to Emma's inquisitor.

It was not funny to Emma, though. The remark set her off. *"WHAT? I have done NOTHING wrong – and I will be out of here shortly. I'm sure this will all be cleared up very soon. I am not a criminal,"* she fired back, convincingly determined.

Her cellmates looked at each other and then stared at Emma, shrugged, and slowly went back to their own bunks. They would cast occasional glances at the new roommate, their latest exhibit.

Well, they are leaving me alone, for now, Emma thought. But that blessing was just one side of the coin; if Emma was no longer a diversion for her cellmates, her cellmates were no longer a diversion for Emma. Her thoughts began to drift. But then her mind was jarred out of its anguished reverie. *"Lights out in five minutes, ladies!"* the guards announced, and true to their warning, exactly five minutes later, Emma and her cellmates, along with hundreds of other inmates throughout the jail, were plunged into darkness.

"Lord, why are you doing this to me?" she softly prayed into the emptiness. *"I am so confused, I don't understand! Get me out of here."*

The only answer that seemed to come was the impersonal ticking of the clock. Eventually, Emma drifted into a troubled, fitful sleep, her emotional and physical exhaustion finally overpowering her racing mind. Waking up frequently and tossing from side to side was the best she could do. It was cold in that jailhouse, and the thin sheet barely covered her entire body.

Every time she closed her eyes that night, she was back in her van seeing the flashing police lights. The last dream was different; this time she was alone in a dark room, being questioned by someone who was very intimidating.

Suddenly Emma heard a voice calling her. She bolted upright in alarm. As her eyes cleared, she saw the jail clock reading 4:45 a.m., but that was not where her attention was fixed. A figure was standing at the foot of her bed with eyes of burning fire, fixed on her, and saying with a soft voice: *"Emma, be at peace!"*

Surely her cell mates must be seeing this, Emma thought, but a quick look at their bunks revealed that they were still asleep, undisturbed. When her eyes returned, the figure was gone – but a deep-rooted peace remained.

Now her heart was pounding at full speed, full of adrenaline. *That must be it*, she thought, *an angel has come to take me home. A rescue from unjust imprisonment.* With hope increasing, Emma quickly dropped to her knees beside her bunk and began to pray:

"God, take me from this awful place, and away from these terrible criminals. Don't abandon me in these cold prison walls."

Emma continued in a whispered prayer, anticipating her freedom to soon come. *Soon,* she thought, *I'll be at home with Victorien and the children.*

While there was a growing sense of peace and comfort, the cell doors remained locked, the clock continued ticking, and her cellmates continued sleeping. Emma was still a prisoner, but something had changed inside of her. That brief encounter had planted a sense of peace and trust that somehow, this ordeal *would* end.

As the days of imprisonment continued, when she began again to worry and sink into depression, she would recall that peaceful voice that softly spoke her name.

The next day, the atmosphere between Emma and her roommates had grown markedly friendlier. Emma began to open up, sharing more about her family and situation. As they listened and interacted, something about these women intrigued Emma. Hearing about their upbringings and life struggles caused Emma to feel sympathy for these criminals. One woman had been charged with drug possession and child neglect, and the other had been arrested for prostitution. In contrast, Emma had never been in trouble with the law and had a family that loved one another. She told these inmates all about them. It sure beat the soul-numbing routine that defined their existence in the Dane County Jail.

After three nights, with no explanation from the authorities, two guards came to the cell to collect Emma.

"Wawa?" one gruff voice asked.

"Right here." Emma answered.

"Get your stuff," a guard ordered, impatient with her slow response. *"Come on. Let's go!"*

Emma, with a sense of surety smiled at her cellmates.

"You're getting outta here girl," one of the women nodded.

The guards, however, did not share the celebration. *"Hurry it up."*

"Hey, be nice to her," the other inmate defended. *"She ain't done nothin' wrong."*

The guards were not about to take any aggravation. *"Shut your mouth, smart a**,"* one of them retorted.

Emma didn't like the edgy turn this was taking and pleaded, *"Please, please, please – stop! Ladies . . . please?"*

In the angry moment of silence that followed, Emma added calmly, *"Thank you, ladies; you'll both be in my prayers."*

Emma turned to the guards and left the cell in which she had been for three days. Flanked by her jailers, she was escorted down that long dark hallway and back into the elevator.

Victorien! Kids! I'm coming home, she thought.

When the elevator doors opened, Emma's visions of a reunion with her family evaporated. Instead of gaining freedom, she was pushed into another holding cell.

Emma looked desperately at the guard sitting at a desk outside the tiny cell. *"Excuse me,"* she said, forcing into her voice a sense of decorum. *"What is going on* here? Why am I back in this cell? Aren't I going home? Where is my husband?"

There was no give in the guard's abrupt response. *"I don't know - but you need to cool that attitude."*

Redoubling her effort to be polite, Emma asked, *"I would just like to know why I have to wait in here?"*

There was a growing anger in the guard's voice now. *"Ma'am, you really need to calm down or there's going to be a problem!"*

This holding cell had a phone, but the inmate-use code that jailers had given her didn't work. She felt even more isolated now, not only being among hostile strangers but unable to tell Victorien what was happening to her.

Finally, she decided to ask the desk guard once more. Despite her patient explanation, he was not in a mood to listen - and he made that abundantly clear.

*"Hey! News flash b****, I don't care!"* he snapped. *"It's not my job to be your assistant. Just try calling again - that's all the help I can give you."*

Emma tried and tried to no avail. She was frightened and overwhelmed. The need to hear Victorian's voice grew deeper as the minutes ticked by. *Why is this so difficult? I just want to talk to my husband,* she thought.

Moments later, Emma saw two guards approaching. Their uniforms were labeled with the words "Dodge County." Her heart sank and she went weak in the knees, remembering the officer's words: *Maximum security. Ninety days. Deportation.* The realization coursed through her veins like ice water. Panic came in waves as the holding cell doors opened, and the two officers quickly shackled Emma hand and foot. She was prodded onto a prisoners' bus. It left the parking lot. Tears spilled. Her heart wept. Madison – and everyone and everything Emma loved there – was shrinking into the distance. The unknown loomed large on the horizon.

Chapter Four

Family Ties: From Africa to America

All of life's events, situations, and trials have led to *this* moment. Paying dearly for her testimony, Emma truly understands who Father God has destined her to be.

As a young girl growing up in Ivory Coast, a small country on the western shore of Africa, Emma had nineteen siblings; six her father had with her mother, and the remainder by his three other wives. Eating as a family always proved to be quite an event. Emma would help her mother by gathering the ingredients and assisting with the preparations. One of her favorite foods to make was peanut butter soup. It was a thick, rich, savory blend of peanut butter, vegetables, and spices that many in her family considered a comfort food.

It was always expected that each family member would make a contribution to the good of the whole, and

Emma most certainly did her part. Sometimes she would pick up other duties that were not her responsibility in an effort to keep everything in order.

The family enjoyed music, games, dancing, and rituals to honor ancestors, while thanking God for blessing the crops and children.

Her father, a nurse by profession, did his best to provide. Near the end of his life diabetes claimed his eyesight, and Emma often helped tend to his needs after school and spend time with him.

Being raised in Agboville's largely Catholic community, Emma naturally had a hunger to know more about God and would regularly attend Sunday Mass as a girl. While she was studying to become a nurse's aide, she visited a home Bible group where she accepted Christ and was baptized at the age of 17.

One day while on a bus home from school, a young man approached her, curious.

"Hi," he said, and Emma cautiously acknowledged him. *"Can I sit there?"* smiling and indicating the empty seat next to her.

Emma clearly hesitated, but that didn't stop this eager young man. Keeping her tone disinterested, Emma, now 20, finally nodded.

"Well," she sighed. *"There ARE a lot of empty seats on this bus, but if you want to sit there, then go ahead. Sit."*

This young man spoke for the entire duration of the bus ride, barely giving Emma a chance to respond. Emma sat and waited for her stop. When it finally came, he followed her off the bus and actually had the nerve to ask for her address. He indicated the prospect of writing her, and she replied, *"If that's what you want to do, then write to me."* Not expecting anything more to come of the encounter, she wrote her address on a piece of paper and went her way.

After a week passed without hearing from him, it wasn't a letter that showed up at Emma's door, it was the young man himself.

"What are YOU doing here?" Emma demanded. *"We don't allow boys in this home."* He smiled and went away with a grin, but there was no escape for Emma on

the bus the next day; he was persistent. During those rides Emma softened and began conversing with this eager young man. Sometime later, a letter did arrive, and it read:

Over the past seveal months I have thoroughly enjoyed my time with you on the bus. Seeing you and sitting with you, even for just a moment, has brightened my life. I wanted to write and let you know about my decision for Christ. When you would speak about Him I felt something genuine and decided that I had to find out for myself, and I am doing that. I would very much like to see you again, and hopefully you feel the same. Thank you for helping me find my way. You are an exceptionally lovely woman.

The letter was signed: *Victorien Wawa.*

Before romance, friendship grew. The letters flew both ways, rich with passion and encouragement. Eventually Victorien shared his feelings about wanting Emma to be his wife. Emma had grown fond of his playful charm, his boundless enthusiasm, and the intensity of his convictions. She was convinced that he was "The One," and the two were engaged. It would be a long engagement - twelve years!

During that time, Victorien decided to move to the United States to further his education, while Emma completed her schooling and worked in Ivory Coast as a nurse. A month after Emma's visa application was granted, she came to New York and married Victorien. They lived in Brooklyn, New York, for four years, where Victorien worked several jobs in restaurants.

In January 1995, their first child, a daughter named Sephora, was born. In December of the same year, Emma gave birth to a son named Eleazar. Shortly after, they decided to move to Wisconsin where some friends had moved and reported that it was a better environment for raising a family, as Victorien had been the victim of muggins in the big city. They were once again embarking on a new journey together.

Once in Wisconsin, they found an apartment in Madison. Victorien was ambitious and quickly found a job in the catering business. Emma nurtured her young children, and shorty thereafter, a third child was born -- a daughter, Deborah. Victorien called her his "princess."

As the family continued to grow, the Wawa's realized that Wisconsin was now home. They desired to become permanent residents. So with their lawyer's help, they made sure to take the necessary legal action. They knew this process wouldn't happen overnight, but they were prepared to do whatever was required of them to become official legal citizens.

With their family thriving, they needed even more space for their energetic children. Emma had always dreamed of owning a home, and after being in Madison for nearly ten years, Victorien was ready to make that dream come true. They began the search for the perfect house and eventually found just the right one. After all of the paperwork and legalities, the Wawas were home owners. It was a beautiful ranch-style house with four bedrooms and plenty of space for a home business (Emma hoped to one day start a daycare).

All this time, the Wawas' desire to reach their friends, co-workers and relatives for Christ had been growing. After much prayer and counsel, they decided to launch the first French-speaking church in Madison out of their home fellowship. The inaugural service was set for Sunday, October 1, 2006. With support from friends and the noteably small French speaking community, Emma and Victorien were excited to once again pioneer another adventure together.

So, when Emma was jailed two weeks prior the launch of the French church, Victorien was confused. Not sure what to do, he sought the Lord, who directed him to stay with the original plan. This was a hard decision for him. Victorien questioned God: *Why would You tell us to start this ministry, then allow Emma to be taken away from me just before we open the doors? This was the vision You gave us together!*

Chapter Five

Out of the Frying Pan, Into the Fire

It was 9 p.m. on September 18, 2006, when the prisoners' bus rolled into the Dodge County Detention Facility in Juneau, Wisconsin. The doors buzzed open and the guards emptied the bus, taking Emma into the jail's maximum-security processing wing. They shoved her into a small interrogation room and left her alone, frightened, and chained.

The room was dimly lit, leaving everything in deep shadows. Two officers scrambled into the room, looking at Emma with little interest. One of the men, apparently the chief, spoke to her, reciting in a near monotone what he called "The Rules."

"Welcome to the Dodge County Detention Facility. This is a maximum-security detention facility

designed for people who have trouble making good decisions," he said firmly. *"In my prison you will obey and respect every superior officer. If you break the rules in ANY way, there will be severe consequences."*

He paused briefly, shot Emma a glance of disdain and demanded: *"Is that UNDERSTOOD?"*

"Yes, Sir," Emma answered.

"Good!" he sneered, as he began thumbing through a file of documents. *"Oh-kaaay,"* he continued, matter-of-factly, *"So, you're an illegal alien. I can tell you that your stay here won't be long as they usually deport illegals pretty d*** quick around here, so . . "*

Though exhausted from her ordeal and trip, that statement nonetheless elicited an energetic response from Emma. She resolutely corrected the prison chief, looking him directly in the eye. *"I am NOT going to be deported,"* she said.

The chief looked at Emma, diverted from the routine he had become used to in processing new inmates held on federal immigration warrants. He met Emma's gaze and replied, *"What did you just say to me?"*

"I am not going to be deported. I do not accept those words, Sir," she said, stronger this time.

Quickly, the chief, with a smirk on his face said, *"Well, well, well."* Becoming mockingly sarcastic, *"Looks to me like we got 'Kunta Kinte' straight outta Africa!"* The nearby guard dutifully laughed at his boss's joke.

Then, the feigned good nature quickly disappeared. *"Understand this you miserible f*** - I don't give a s*** what happens to you,"* the chief growled. *"Don't interrupt me again, understand?"*

This time, Emma was silent, simply nodding that, yes, she most certainly understood.

Satisfied he had asserted his authority over this helpless little African woman shackled in the chair before him, the chief continued leafing through Emma's file.

"OK. Got picked up. . . spent the last part of the week in the Dane County Jail. . . And now you're here."

He looked again at Emma. *"What exactly did the judge rule in your case?"* he asked.

"I haven't committed any crime, and I haven't been to see any judge," she answered. *"Look at me, I'm tied to this chair, in this dark room, it's late and I can barely even see your face. Shouldn't my lawyer be present at these kinds of meetings?"*

At least she's not boring, not just another run-of-the-mill hooker, drug addict, check bouncer or thief. Why, this could be interesting, he thought.

"Wawa," he snickered. *"The fact is, you are an ILLEGAL alien in the U.S.A., and lawyer or not, that's a crime. When you break a law in this country, you get punished."*

Emma protested, refusing to buckle. She repeated that she had broken no law for what seemed over the past days to be the hundredth time. Immigration paperwork had arrived regularly at their Madison address – and they had dutifully responded to it. INS obviously knew where she lived, so how could she be "running," as she was being accused?

"What is my crime?" she asked. *"You tell me, what is it? How is it that I am in a maximum-security prison?"*

This game was no longer entertaining for the jailers, and this particular inmate's insistence on her innocence was becoming disconcerting for them. *Enough,* the chief decided, bellowing over Emma's protests.

"WAWA! I don't want to listen to this s***. I don't make the god d***ed rules for Immigration, and they sure as h*** aren't going to change for you," he snapped. *"Inmates here on Immigration charges are deported within ninety days, usually sooner, and that's that!"*

He continued, a bit calmer in tone: *"I haven't seen a single inmate with immigration issues ever get released."*

Fresh tears erupted from Emma's bloodshot eyes. *"Can I please call my husband? He doesn't even know I'm here,"* she asked.

The jailer looked at his watch, at first saying it was too late, but then, nodding to the guard accompanying him, he reluctantly decided to show a shred of compassion.

"Make it quick," he said.

"Thank you, Sir," Emma said as the guard led her out of the room to a bank of telephones. The chief made no reply and picked up Emma's file again, puzzled as he read the documents with renewed interest.

Emma found comfort in dialing the familiar numbers and hearing the phone ring. Then, she heard his voice. *"Hello?"* Victorien answered.

Erupting to an instant sob, Emma began, *"Oh Victorien, they brought me to Dodge County prison and say that I only have ninety days before I am deported."*

"Oh, God," he said, trying to compose himself. *"Listen, I don't know what is going to happen but I love you and will do whatever needs to be done to get you home. We must trust and believe that you will be released."* He paused, and there was a moment of silence. They realized that their faith was being put to the test and what they truly believed was on the line. He asked her again, *"Do you trust Him, Emma?"*

Her optimism was diminishing, and she could not in good faith directly answer that question.

"Victorien, I do not belong in prison. I didn't do anything wrong. I don't deserve this!" she cried.

"I know, Sweetie, you didn't do anything wrong," Victorien assured her.

She asked why their lawyer hadn't called or come. Victorien informed her of the situation -- that he was in the process of finding a new lawyer. When Emma asked how they were going to pay this new attorney, Victorien had some good news. Their parent church, Evangel Life Center, had offered to help with the fees.

He told her of one attorney's suggestion to have family and friends write a flood of letters to encourage Emma. Those notes were likely already in the mail.

The couple quickly caught up on more domestic matters. The children missed their mom; her absence touched every area of their lives from the food she prepared for them to the bedtime prayers and all the joy she brought into their home. From time to time, Victorien would attempt to lightenen the mood by telling them that "Mama's jail cell is a very nice one, like a hotel room" and "Mama is meeting lots of interesting people who have some crazy stories to tell her" and, of course, "Mama will be home soon."

The anecdote was Victorien's attempt at humor that he hoped might ease his wife's somber mood. He could hear that this approach wasn't working when he heard Emma weeping on the other end of the line. Victorien began to pray: *Lord, please comfort my wife. She needs You! Show her comfort and mercy. Please work swiftly to reunite our family. Help us to trust You each day. Oh God, we need a miracle.*

Victorien got as much information from Emma about her condition as he could, knowing this conversation would end all too soon. Those moments together on the phone brought some relief and strength to each of them. He told her about the launch of the French church, and she was glad he had decided to go ahead with their original plan. Victorien begged her to let him come, but she would not, for if he came, they could arrest him on the same charges. Their children would end up in foster care – a scenario Emma refused to accept.

The ten-minute call seemed like it had lasted only seconds. Emma's moment of respite was over.

Within minutes, Emma was alone inside another cold cell. Weary and drained, Emma laid in the dark under a thin sheet on a flimsy mattress, and drifting into another fitful, troubled sleep.

Chapter Six

Imprisoned with Purpose

"Our level of confidence in God," she says, *"depends on how well we know Him."*

"If I was about to meet your father, and you had to explain to me what he was like, what kinds of things would you describe?" Emma pauses. *"When we introduce people to our heavenly Father, we must know intimately and with passion Who we are introducing."*

In the Dodge County's maximum-security unit, Emma's days had become a merciless grind that drained her mind and spirit. Loud buzzers heralded breakfast, lunch, and dinner. Harsh voices over the prison's speakers announced cell searches and inspections, roll calls, and "lights out."

Prison life consisted of the unending smell of stale, rancid sweat, the sickening stench of clogged toilets, and angry expressions of women who had lost hope. Emma never got used to it. It was too much to accept, even when she felt like she could no longer keep track of the hours that dripped into days.

Emma had now been at Dodge County for almost two weeks and was receiving the letters Victorien had mentioned. They helped some, those notes of encouragement from her friends, but they were just interludes to the long days and nights behind bars. Two visits from her pastors had lifted her spirits. They would bring notes and messages from Victorien and the family. On their second visit, they delivered her French Bible and some money for her jail account to buy things like soap and other personal items.

Emma tried her best to stay out of the spotlight. If she kept quiet, then no one would bother her, she thought. It had worked so far, and she wasn't about to change the plan now.

A common room was used as the unit's cafeteria and was filled with strangers who all seemed like hard, tough women. There was no welcome there, where pockets of inmates gathered in cliques, eyeing newcomers with cold disdain.

When it was time to eat, Emma would look for an empty table and cautiously make her way to it. This had become her routine until one day when two guards noisily burst into the cafeteria and ordered *Emma Wawa* to accompany them to the unit's office. They looked around and waited for her to identify herself. The room quieted down and all the inmates stared at her as she hastily made her way through the cafeteria. In the office she was given a new uniform, told to change, retrieve her belongings, and report back.

As she shed her green jail uniform and put on the new yellow one, Emma noticed looks of concern growing among her cellmates.

"Hey, why are you in yellow?" one woman remarked.

Emma replied, *"They just told me to put it on, get my things, and come right back."*

When Emma returned, she asked the desk guard for an explanation. He laughed, then shrugged, *"Immigration wants us to classify you as a hard criminal. You'll have to wear yellow for two weeks in lockdown, and then they'll evaluate you."*

Emma's face drooped in disbelief. *Hard Criminal*, she thought. The guard noticed her confused response and added, *"After you've been a 'good girl' they'll give your privileges back."*

Lockdown? What privileges was she about to lose? What had she done to deserve this?

"Yep, it's hard time for you Wawa," the guard continued, *"No visitors. No phone calls. No activities. No roommates. No . . . nothing."*

It suddenly dawned on her: She would be cut off from everything, even her weekly priceless conversations with Victorien. *"No phone calls?"* she whispered.

"Two weeks," the guard nodded.

Officers came and escorted Emma to her new solitary cell. Numb and confused, she sat on her metal cot for several hours in pure frustration, questioning everything. *This is the most unfair, undeserving treatment I have ever received and for what? Paying my taxes? Filing all of these legal documents? Faithfully meeting the stringent requirements of Immigration? Doing everything by-the-book?* It then got personal with the Lord. *Is this how You treat Your daughters? Is this the reward of a faithful servant? Is this what I get for serving You? Are You trying to ruin my life?*

Her mind was troubled for several days as her emotions began to take control of her spirit. She felt her life was spinning out of control, tumbling into darkness and then into a fear-filled abyss. Fueled with anger, Emma rolled in and out of sleep, unaware of the time.

On the third day of her solitary stay, an abrupt shout rolled into her dark thoughts: *"EMMA! Wake up!"*

"Who is there?" she whispered, peering into the mist of her mind, even as those clouds of terror seemed to quiet and slowly dissipate.

"Emma. It's time for your retreat," the voice declared and tenderly added, *"Don't you remember?"*

Emma's mind scrolled, and she suddenly recalled the last church service that she attended before getting arrested. She remembered telling Victorien that she needed a retreat, alone with God, away from everything, before the launch of the French church.

"Yes, I remember," she answered. Emma stood up with tears welling in her eyes, obediently accepting a gift she no longer wanted.

"This is not what I had in mind when I asked for a retreat," she thought as she instantly recalled the next statement she had made, *"I am going to live for You with a one-hundred percent commitment, from now on. One-hundred percent, no less."*

A newly birthed passion for the upcoming launch of the French church was on the forefront of Emma's mind when she had declared these things, but that didn't void the fact that she had made this declaration to her heavenly Father.

She was going to have eleven more days to contemplate these things.

And so it was on a retreat, alone with God – just not the get-away she had envisioned. The days consisted of routine: sitting, standing, pacing, sleeping, eating, crying, praying, singing, laughing and kneeling. There was the anxious pouring out of fears and doubts followed by peace, confidence, and eventually joy in the presence of God.

Emma was getting a heavenly deposit for her next task at hand. She knew this was necessary, but at the same time it was terribly difficult and lonely. It would be early November soon, and the children were getting ready for their fall field trips. Victorien would soon be humming Christmas songs. She thought of them and asked God to bring them the same peace and revelation that He was bringing to her.

On the second-to-last day of her "retreat," she asked God what His plans were for her while she was in prison. He began to show her that His purpose for her imprisonment was not for her punishment. No, that was not it at all. Instead, there were broken lives in those prison walls that desperately needed a spiritual lifeline, and she would be His hand extended. Those last two days seemed only a moment.

Emma was taken into an interrogation room and placed in front of a panel of officers. It was hard to make out their faces through the poorly lit space. She had been in a cell where the lights blarred for fourteen days straight. She did recognize one voice: the prison chief.

As she waited, the sound of whispers and shuffling papers filled the small room.

"Hello, Wawa. How have you been?" he asked, the sarcasm dripping from his voice. *"You ready to start behaving?"*

She simply answered, *"Yes, sir,"* and the response seemed to please the chief. If she could not clearly see the expression on his face, she could still sense the gloating.

"Good," he said, telling her she would soon shed the yellow uniform for a new green one and would be put into a unit with ten other prisoners.

"You will eat, sleep, shower and s*** with these animals," he said, seemingly proud of his crude speech. *"Is that going to be a problem, Wawa?"* the chief added with an undertone of menace in his voice.

"No, sir."

He paused to dismiss her but had one more inquiry.

"Wawa, you got a s*** load of mail last week! Why are you so popular?" he asked.

Emma told him that the letters were from her family at church. They totaled more than sixty in all.

"Hmmph. Well, it's all waiting for you in the pad," he said, then nodding to a nearby guard. *"Make sure she finds a shower on the way, she reeks! Get her outta here,"* he barked, no longer amused by the conversation.

In the shower, Emma only had one thing on her mind: to call home. Once in her new pad, she found the phone and dialed Victorien. They spoke for nearly an hour about everything that had taken place in the past two weeks in solitary. He had become very worried and angry that no one could tell him where she was or why he was unable to speak with her. She told him all about her encounter with the Lord and what her purpose was going to be as long as she was in prison. Hearing this, Victorien's attitude shifted. He now viewed his wife as an ambassador for Christ rather than a victim of "the system."

Victorien had good and bad news from the lawyer. The good news was that they had filed all the necessary appeals and those were now in play. The bad news was, for a reason that would forever remain unknown to them, their previous lawyer had failed to file several important documents when they moved into their new house. Even after hearing this, Emma was not frightened; she even encouraged Victorien to have faith in God's plan and not in his own reasoning. She declared that she would be released; getting deported was not in the plan.

Victorien was instantly filled with faith and encouragement after their talk and immediately gathered the children and told them the good news. From that point on, every Saturday night, Victorien would lay an outfit on their bed, anticipating Emma would be home to wear it to church the next day. The kids would ask him why he did that, and he would always reply, "We want to be ready when she returns."

Emma collected her mail. These letters contained drawings from children at church, pictures friends took of her own children, updates on current events, and scriptures to encourage her. In her new pad, she noticed a woman sitting alone and thought, *It is time.*

Emma walked to the table and sat down. Their eyes met as she introduced herself. Emma hoped this first attempt to 'reach out' wouldn't land her a black eye or worse. Instead, the woman plainly asked, *"So, why are you here?"*

"Because the Lord has placed me here," Emma replied, not knowing what would come next.

"I haven't heard that one before. What the hell did you do, steal from the plate or something?" the woman replied.

Emma responded gently and honestly, *"I was brought here on Immigration issues."*

"Oh. They want to deport you," the inmate said.

"Well," Emma sighed, "That is what they say, but this is not what God has for me!"

The answer took the woman by surprise. "Oh . . . . Hangin' on to Jesus, eh?"

"Yes, I am," Emma remarked boldly.

The conversation took its seemingly scripted course. Emma explained that at first the cop who pulled her over thought she was drunk because her van had swerved. She was just tired, she explained to the officer, who believed her. He was even about to let her go – until his routine check on her license and Social Security card turned up an immigration warrant for her arrest.

"Wow, I never thought I'd get to meet a real terrorist!" Emma's tablemate joked, and they both laughed. Then, more seriously, the woman added, "You know they're deporting people outta here every week, don't you?"

Emma's face remained calm. *"It seems that way, but I truly believe that being deported is not God's will for my life,"* she said.

The tablemate gave Emma a look of disbelief and said, *"I guess to each his own. Everybody in here b****es, especially about the people that put 'em in here, but you don't seem angry. We'll see if that lasts for you."*

The woman gestured to a group of Hispanic inmates, *"Look at them, I'll bet you they'll all be deported by the end of the month. S*** they might as well already be gone. Tell me, how is God gonna save your black a**?"*

Emma didn't appreciate the language or hostility. She took a moment and then calmed her reaction. Instead of responding with anger, Emma realized this woman needed love and not another contender to fight against. So, Emma began to share her faith just as she had done many times before, even with her own husband.

The woman introduced herself after Emma had shared her personal testimony. *"Well, I'm Emily. I just got transferred from Pad D because of some differences of opinion with some of the other inmates. Where are you bunked?"* she asked.

They went on with conversation, and Emma kindly asked Emily why she had to use that language all the time.

Emily answered, *"You really ARE a saint, huh? Someone in here who doesn't say f*** every other word . . . hmm. Tell you what, I'll watch my cussin' around you."*

Emma nodded and replied with an equal sincerity. *"Well, I guess I shouldn't assume that everyone in here has experienced the power of Jesus yet."*

As the two laughed at the table a connection was made. Emma now saw Emily not as a hard criminal but as someone who needed a friend. She asked, *"What about you? Do you know the real Jesus?"*

Emily shrugged. *"Me...? I went to church as a girl,"* she said.

"But do you know the Father and the love He has for you?" Emma asked.

Emily looked down, silent for a moment, and then slowly looked into Emma's warm and welcoming eyes. Tenderly she replied, *"I wish I did. My father hated me."*

As tears began to roll down Emily's face at the table, grace fell from heaven. Emma prayed: *Lord, thank You for providing our every need. You are the One who holds us in your arms. We thank you for being our Father and that Your love is unconditional and never ends.* As they prayed, two inmates approached the table and asked what was going on.

"We're talking about Jesus." Emma replied and then quickly asked, *"Well, do you know Him?"*

"Oh, s***. Are you some kind of preacher? Weren't you in lockdown?" the woman snorted. *"Yeah, the Bible study was yesterday,"* the other inmate chimed in with a laugh.

Decidedly unoffendable, Emma answered, *"That's OK. It doesn't matter what people think about me. Immigration wanted me to be processed as a hard criminal so they gave me a yellow uniform, and I was all by myself in a cell for the past two weeks. And it was a long two weeks – but now, I'm ready."*

Emma continued talking with the small group of women and skillfully steered the conversation toward heaven. To her surprise, they could actually recite many Bible stories. Why, one of their own cousins was a minister.

"So, is Jesus the centerpiece of your heart?" Emma politely interrupted one of the women.

With a mix of amusement, confusion and uncertainty, their answer was "No."

"I said a prayer once, but that was long ago when I was young and happy. Now, I'm just an inmate," one of them replied.

Emma explained that knowing Jesus is so much more than reciting a prayer. *"It's a life-changing relationship,"* she said. *"Everyone has a choice, regardless of what they have done."*

The woman gestured toward a group of tough looking women at another table and said, *"Murderers, lesbians, drug dealers and whores, what about them?"*

Yes, Emma nodded, all of them. *"No one is too bad for God. Each person must make their own decision. I am only capable of making choices for myself,"* she said.

The two women were hungry for answers. *"How do you know there is a God?"* they asked.

She told them about how she had seen God's glory while in solitary confinement, been ministered to by angels and immersed in His presence. She had felt His touch and heard His voice, even behind bars.

"Ladies, if you don't see Him it's because you are not looking. When you open your eyes, you can experience all of these things," she concluded.

When the guard announced it was time for lunch, Emma found herself with three new friends as she shuffled into the serving line. Emily, Miranda and Jessie proceeded to try to tell Emma how things worked: which of the inmates were dangerous, which were all right to talk to, which ones to avoid. She paid especially close attention when a nearby group of Hispanic women was pointed out.

"They're like you, here on Immigration charges. They're pretty nice, but don't fight with them 'cause they'll all jump you. They usually aren't here for very long, and after they go to Chicago, we never see 'em again. Once you go there, it's bye-bye America," Miranda explained.

The three of them found a table and began eating.

"So, what I try to do when I'm eating this slop is hold my breath," Miranda smiled. *"It goes down easier that way."*

Jessie added, laughing: *"Yeah. It's kinda like dog food . . . only worse."*

Emma took part in the good-natured banter, but as they ate she couldn't help the feeling of unease inside as she watched the Hispanic women, thinking that they would soon be deported. *Chicago. Once you go there, it's bye-bye America.*

Back at her cot, Emma's purpose was now clearer than ever. She quietly prayed in French as she closed her eyes that night.

"Lord, you have given me purpose. Help me to clearly hear Your voice when You speak to me. I trust You with everything I have, completely. Forgive me for judging these women, and let me be a light for You in this cold, dark prison."

Chapter Seven

A Ticket to Ride -- on a Spiritual Roller Coaster

After several weeks, Emma wasn't the new fish in the prison pond anymore. An unfamiliar inmate had arrived. Clad in an orange uniform of the freshly booked, she was sitting alone at a table in the common room. The woman leafed through a magazine in an attempt to hide her discomfort. As Emma walked by, their eyes met.

"Hi, I'm Goldie. What are you here for?" she asked.

Well of course, Emma thought, *I could write the script for introductions in prison, couldn't I? It's always the first question, one inmate to another.*

"Immigration," Emma answered, fighting the urge to sigh.

"*Deportation?*" Goldie responded, another question.

Here we go again, Emma thought.

"*Well my God has another plan for me - and in the name of Jesus, I refuse to believe that it will be deportation!*" she countered, with edge in her voice.

Goldie rocked back in her seat, then said with a hint of awe, "*Oooo. I like that.*"

"*What? You like . . . what?*" Emma said. Now it was her turn to be a little confused.

"*What you just said. I like that,*" Goldie explained, and then suddenly began to sob, her attempts to look and act tough shattering.

Emma's heart melted. She felt that familiar spirit of love well up inside her and acknowledged that this was yet another opportunity to encourage and comfort. Emma moved to the table and sat down beside Goldie.

"*I . . . I messed up. BIG TIME,*" Goldie whispered. "*I started using and dealing drugs. I knew it was wrong, but I thought it was what I wanted. Once I got busted, I realized that I needed some serious help. I prayed and told God that I didn't want this life anymore,"* she added, tears flowing freely. *"I'm so TIRED of this life! Tired of my family being divided. Tired of my kids being taken away. Tired of drugs ruling my life."*

"Wow," Emma said, as amazed at God arranging this encounter as she was at the genuine regret lacing Goldie's story. *"Goldie, God likes it when you're honest with Him."*

Goldie looked into Emma's eyes and asked, *"Why are you being so nice to me?"*

"Because my Father has sent me here to love you," Emma replied.

Goldie began to recount how she had specifically prayed and asked God to send a strong Christian into her life. *"You are the answer to my prayer,"* she added. *"God has ANSWERED my prayer. This is so incredible!"*

Soon the two were laughing together at the table. Emma learned that Goldie had applied for a drug rehabilitation program offered by an organization called

Teen Challenge. Facing a possible maximum prison term of 25 years, she needed a compassionate judge to have a chance at acceptance to the program.

"Father, I lift up my friend Goldie and her situation to You," Emma prayed. *"Thank You for Your compassion and forgiveness. If it is Your will that Goldie would attend Teen Challenge, then please speak to the judge and be with him as he makes his ruling."*

Emma went to sleep that night happy, excited that once again the Lord had used her ordeal for good.

But the peaceful slumber lasted only for a brief time. At 3 a.m., guards loudly stormed over to Emma's cot.

"Get up, Wawa," they ordered. Hauled into an interrogation room, Emma's gaze met the familiar, unpleasant face of the prison chief under the harsh lights.

"Sign the papers," he demanded, pointing to a stack of forms.

"What are these papers?" Emma answered, confused but heeding a swelling sense of alarm and warning.

"Just . . . sign . . . the . . . D*** PAPERS!" he hollered.

By now Emma's mind was clearing, her initial fright being supplanted by determination.

"Where is my lawyer?" she asked, setting down the pen that had been forced to her palm. She sat up straight, squared her shoulder and insisted, *"No. I am NOT going to sign anything until my lawyer is present."*

The chief, frustrated that his bullying had failed, growled: *"Jee-suss Christ, Wawa! Why can't you just cooperate?"*

Emma held back the urge to slap his face, deciding it was now the jail chief who would be answering questions – and she would be the one asking them.

"Why do you startle me awake in the middle of the night? Shine lights in my face, bring me into this dark

room and try to force me to sign these papers I have never seen? I do not trust you!" she demanded, feeling strangely empowered.

The tactics of intimidation had failed. But the chief thought he had one more card to play that would surely pummel this feisty immigrant.

He lowered himself and got right in her face, so close their noses were almost touching, and said, *"Fine! You're goin' to Chicago, Wawa. Mark my words you cocky b****. I'm deporting you!"*

He turned to the nearby guards who had brought her down. *"Get her s*** together and put her on the bus,"* he shouted as the officers put her in shackles. Emma began to weep softly.

The bus was packed with a variety of other immigrants, and Emma heard several languages being spoken. She was the only one shackled. As the bus jerked out of the prison, Emma closed her exhausted eyes and slid into the blackness of an uneasy sleep.

As she sat on the bus she recalled a verse from Isaiah 19 and clung to it with all her might.

It will be a sign and witness to the LORD Almighty. When they cry out to the Lord because of their oppressors, he will send them a savior and defender, and he will rescue them.

She claimed that promise and whispered a quick petition to God, *"Lord, be with me!"*

The three-hour ride from Juneau to Chicago seemed never ending, but the bus eventually rolled into downtown Chicago. A guard shouted at the inmates, *"Wake up, ladies; we're just about there."*

They were herded off the bus into a gray, cold, triangular skyscraper of a prison where a new set of guards shifted them into a processing area. There were patrols stationed at every exit with assault rifles and combat gear, as if a war ensued. Before long a self-important, well-dressed officer made his way forward with a clipboard in hand.

"OK, everyone – listen up!" he demanded, as the eyes of the women snapped to attention. *"This is it, you're being deported."*

The officer instructed, pointing to a camera station and a waiting photographer, *"Right here is where you're going to get your picture taken. After that, you'll come back over here and we'll process your deportation papers. Once everything is ready, you'll wait a bit, and then we'll put you on a plane."*

Emma's heart began to sink, but she fought the urge to quit and shook her head. *No, this is not what the Lord showed me would happen. I refuse it!* She silently prayed.

Meanwhile, the officer was wrapping up his "welcome" to the immigration prisoners. *"We're gonna try to move everybody through as quickly as possible, but we're NOT gonna tolerate ANY unnecessary behavior. So, if you wanna get BEAT - try something stupid!"*

One by one, the deportees shuffled forward. Click, flash, move on. Women wept, others sighed, still others held their heads down in defeat, but the line inexorably moved forward.

Finally, Emma stood at the front, next in line for her prison portrait.

"Name?" a guard asked.

"Emma Wawa."

The officer leafed through his list. Once. Twice. Perplexed, he looked up at Emma and asked,   " *'Wawa,' you said?"* She nodded.

The guard turned toward the officer in charge and said, *"Hey, boss? I got one that's not on my list!"*

"What?" the officer responded.

"She's NOT on the list," the guard repeated, holding up the sheets of inmates to be deported. The officer grabbed the paperwork himself and spun on Emma. *"What's your name?"* he demanded.

Smiling as if already knowing the outcome, she slowly and clearly enunciated each syllable, *"Em-ma, Wa-wa."*

"What the h*** are you smiling about?" the officer looked at her and asked.

A hurried look through the list yielded no such name. The officer's face reddened as the veins on his face began to rise. *"Oh, what the . . . .!"* Then, recomposing himself, *"Take her picture, anyway. I'll go check this out,"* he ordered.

Emma was pointed to the marked position in front of the camera, her photograph was snapped, and she was put back in line. She watched as more women were moved through the process. Finally, the prison officer returned, telling Emma to follow him to an office. Once there, he picked up a telephone and started dialing.

"You came from Dodge County Jail, right?" he asked. *"Yes, sir,"* Emma replied, politely grinning. The officer nodded and then turned his attention to the phone.

"Yeah," he said into the receiver. *"Chicago Immigration calling. What's with this 'Emma Wawa' you sent me? She's NOT on my list."* He listened for a moment and scowled.

*"What the h***? Don't send me people that aren't on my list,"* he barked, listening some more, then nodding in disgust. *"Well, she may be on your list but she's not on mine. Send your boys back to get her. That's*

right – BECAUSE I'm not deporting someone who's not on my list!" he said, abruptly hanging up. Then he looked at Emma who seemed amused at the conversation.

"You got lucky, Wawa." he said.

Emma could not contain her relief and joy. *"PRAISE the LORD!"* she smiled. *"I KNEW I wouldn't be deported."*

Disbelief, then scorn shadowed the officer's face. *"That ain't God, Wawa. That's just stupid luck,"* he said.

Emboldened by events, Emma retorted: *"I rebuke that, in the name of Jesus."*

Un-be-lievable, the officer's expression seemed to say, then his brow furrowed. *"How about this – when you come back, and you most certainly will, I'll PERSONALLY escort you to your plane. How does THAT sound?"* he mocked.

Emma shook her head. *"No, you won't. I am a daughter of the Most High."*

"Psssh. Whatever," he answered, motioning the guards to take Emma to a small holding cell until her ride back to Dodge County Jail arrived.

During her two hour wait, Emma was allowed to make a quick phone call. It was more than enough time to share a miracle.

Victorien answered, *"Is everything OK? Where are you?"*

Emma told him of the night's events, the long bus ride, the seeming end-of-the-road, and then the reprieve.

"Oh, my Lord, thank You," Victorien said. *"Still, I think I might have just had a small heart attack!"*

Emma laughed. What a relief. She had avoided deportation. *Somehow.*

Chapter Eight

A Spiritual War: Attack and Counterattack

Psalm 91, verse 15: *"He will call upon me, and I will answer him; I will be with him in trouble, I will deliver him and honor him."*

"Choose to look up to Him! He is above every situation," Emma says, gently closing her Bible. *"I do not know what situation you are going through. But I know this: What He has done for me, He can do for you!"*

The opportunities became endless for Emma to share her renewed faith. Having been the first inmate to return to the jail in Dodge County from Chicago, most everyone was amazed, including some of the guards. The prison chief, humiliated, was determined to break Emma. He had just the plan.

Emma's cellmates had, one by one, joined her Bible study. Many had accepted Christ. What began as a mistaken arrest and imprisonment had become Emma's own unique missionary journey. By simply loving the women she encountered, there had been a spiritual harvest in the most unlikely of places. Where hopelessness, regret, and pain had burdened so many souls, the message of forgiveness and love had found fertile ground.

It was now mid-December, and Emma's ninety-day term was coming to an end. With the anticipation of her release, Emma was beginning to see the light at the end of the tunnel, and it couldn't come soon enough.

Hostile jailers were one thing, but hostile inmates were an entirely different story. Emma hadn't dealt personally with any inmate conflicts up until this point. One afternoon while Emma was quietly reading her Bible, the hostile inmate arrived.

"Hey, Wawa! God told me you're going home today!"

"What?"

The new inmate, aggitated, shook her head and muttered, *"You are such a dumb a**."*

"Excuse me," Emma looked at her, aware this woman was clearly upset. *"How do you know my name, and why are you saying these things to me? Is there a problem? . . . ."*

"You were BORN, stupid b****! Just go and . . . pray or something," the woman snapped. *"All this, 'Save me from my sins, Wawa!', 'I need JESUS, Wawa!', 'Tell me about the Bible, Wawa!' I'm sick of hearing that s*** all of the time!"*

As Emma rose to walk away, the inmate shot a glance to a jail supervisor. He nodded approvingly and then faded into the background. Emboldened, the inmate continued to shout more derision at Emma's back.

"Oh, I get it. I'm not good enough to be in your little 'Jesus club.' I guess God hates fags, huh?" she spat out angrily. *"That s*** is so BOGUS!"*

It seemed today was going to spiral. Two guards came in several moments later and transferred Emma to a different pad. There, she was reunited with Emily, Miranda and Jessie.

Emma began to phycially describe the woman she had just encountered and asked her friends if they had ever seen her before, but none of them seemed to. They had many things to ask Emma. One situation needed immediate attention.

"Good thing you're here," Miranda piped up. *"We need you to talk to Michelle; she's losing it, bad."*

Emma's eyes narrowed with concern. *"What's wrong with her?"* she asked.

She had been dealt a heavy prison term by the judge – eighteen years. Emma's inmate sisters had tried to console the crushed woman, but she remained despondent.

Emma quickly stowed her belongings by her cot and went to find Michelle. When she located her, the woman's dark, weary eyes showed a spark of recognition as Emma approached.

As they discussed her sentence, Michelle's demeanor became bitter.

"There is no God," Michelle blurted out. "If there was, He wouldn't have done this to me! I prayed. I went to the Bible study, all of that, and it didn't work. I'm not wasting anymore time praying to a God that doesn't care about me!"

Michelle spilled out her hurt and hopeless anger, insisting it was God's fault that she would be away from her kids while they grew up.

"I'm gonna be an old woman by the time I get outta this s***hole! God abandoned me," she hollered.

As Michelle's rage crumbled into weeping, Emma moved closer and took the sobbing woman in her arms. "He hasn't left you, Michelle. . . . Why don't you try thanking Him?"

"For WHAT?"

"That your sentence wasn't longer." Emma answered softly. "God does not abandon His children. Look at me. Do you know what everyone tells me?

'Wawa, you're going to be deported.' But here I am, back from Chicago," Emma added. "No one has ever returned to Dodge County from Chicago, but I did! God did not abandon about me."

Michelle allowed Emma to pray with her, and as Michelle began to pour out her pain and disappointment to heaven, gradually her anger subsided and hope once more flickered in her eyes.

That evening Emma spoke with Victorien and was anxious for some good news. Her ninety-day stay was only four days away from completion. Victorien certainly brightened the mood of the conversation by suggesting she would be reunited with them for Christmas. Emma asked what Victorien had heard from the lawyer and how the children were doing; the conversation moved nicely. They had a sweet time on the phone that night, knowing their long-awaited embrace was so near.

Back in her new pad, Emma found that this hostile inmate had also been transferred, to the cot directly next to hers. This foul-mouthed prisoner leeringly suggested they *share a bed for the night.* Emma ingored her remarks, held her tongue and rolled over to try and find some sleep. Just as Emma began to relax, the inmate leaned over and whispered a threat.

"Once you fall asleep, Wawa, I'm gonna slit your throat," she said. *"Sweet dreams . . . Never know, maybe God will save you tonight...or not."*

About an hour after Emma had finally fallen asleep, a herd of guards shook her awake and hauled her out of the pad. They alleged that a complaint had been filed stating that Emma was giving one of the new inmates trouble. They questioned her and then left the small room where they had taken her. Emma shook her head and gazed at the concrete ceiling, *"WHAT are you doing, Lord? I have done everything You have asked of me!"*

Emma wiped her eyes and stubbornly decided to maintain a positive attitude. It was an act of will, to be sure. Now, more than ever, she felt that God was with her. She knew that the smallest incident could get her into loads of trouble, which could ultimately lead to deportation. *My purpose,* Emma reminded herself, *is to show all of these women love and encouragement.*

The prison chief burst into the small dark room waiving a letter as he said mockingly, *"Good news, Wawa, you're going to be with us for Christmas, and for ANOTHER ninety days. Isn't that great?"*

"Why?" Emma whispered with a shock, her head reeling. She was told that the letter contained a charge that she had "failed to cooperate" with Immigration officials, and that she would now face allegations of conspiring against the United States government.

Conspiracy?

Allegedly, she had failed to provide a birth certificate or valid Green Card.

"Hey, at least you've got a new roommate to keep you company," the chief smirked, suddenly rising. *"You're going to break, Wawa, another ninety days. . . ho, ho, ho and Merry Christmas."*

As Emma leaned her head to her lap, the chief left the room. Overwhelmed yet again and alone with her racing mind, she struggled to gather her emotions. *How am I going to tell Victorien and the children? Christmas?* In an instant, what had once been so close, was now so far away. *"I have been here for ninety days. How am I going to survive this all over again?"*

She heard nothing as she sat and waited. Only silence. *Christmas in prison,* she thought. It was then, in her spirit, she decided that *victory delayed was not victory denied.*

The next day, through the reinforced glass of the high-security visitation room, Emma smiled as her pastor sat down and picked up the phone. The visits had always come when Emma needed them most. The chief's sneering announcement was a heavy blow, and her family wasn't taking it well. Pastor John Clark kindly informed her that her family would be well taken care of during the Christmas season.

The visits had become a source of encouragement for him also as Emma always had spiritual victories to share: a suicidal cellmate finding a new life in Christ, more women at the Bible studies, not to mention the support, care and love these women now showed each other instead of fighting. She also shared the not-so-good news of her hostile inmate, Teeka.

Pastor Clark laughingly encouraged Emma not to beat up this troubled inmate, and she assured him that if it came to that, she would be deported, because she could surely provide her with a good whooping. It was refreshing to laugh, and Emma always appreciated his humor.

By Emma's request, Pastor Clark had brought money to deposit into her jail account because she had decided to give her fellow cellmates a holiday pizza party. She had explained the idea to Victorien, and Pastor Clark was happy to help out. They prayed together, and Emma retuned to her pad.

On Christmas Eve, after her morning routine, Emma overheard Teeka spewing her hatred for the "African preacher" to Jessie.

"Wawa's a good woman; why are you being so mean to her?" Jessie asked in defense of her friend.

"Maybe there's something in it for me," Teeka quietly boasted. *"If I can get her to break, I'm gonna get some special privileges."*

"What do you mean by 'break her'?" Jessie asked.

"If I can get her in trouble, then I'll get rewarded," Teeka answered.

Emma walked in, her eyes afire. It was now obvious that Teeka was trying to unnerve her with the approval, if not under the direction, of the prison officials.

"Now it makes sense," Emma declared, moving within inches of Teeka's face. *"Go ahead and play your games; I am not scared of you, and I most certainly will not be deported! Don't you know that I am a daughter of the Most High God?"*

Stunned, silenced, and defeated, Teeka left the room. Jessie had just watched Emma unmask this conflict with a gracious confidence, void of anger but full of authority. Emma thanked Jessie for defending her and declared that this curse was now broken.

Carrying several boxes of pizza, Emma announced to the ladies in the pad that she had a gift for all of them. She made a point of inviting the now withdrawn Teeka to share as well. Shocked, the hardened woman's face seemed to lose its hostility as Emma handed her a slice.

"*OK, ladies . . . . how's the pizza?*" Emma asked the happy, mouth-filled crowd. She was answered with a boisterous chorus of approval.

Emma smiled and nodded. "*Well, I want to share something with you tonight. You all know that I trust Jesus with my life and sometimes that can be very hard. . . . I found out this week that I am going to be here for another ninety days. To me, that can only mean that my job here is not yet finished.*"

Emily, Miranda, Jessie, and Teeka, as well as a dozen other inmates paused, looks of sympathy and shock giving way to an increased attention to Emma's words.

"*God has a plan for each of us,*" Emma continued. "*I don't understand His ways, but I choose to follow Him. It is Christmas Eve tonight, and none of us are at home. I must admit, I would love to be with my family right now, but, as it so happens, I am with a different family. So, the first gift I have for you is the pizza, and the second is the story of my Savior's birth.*"

She shared the simple, timeless story. How the Holy Spirit had come upon the virgin Mary. The heavenly reassurance given to her husband-to-be, Joseph, that he should take her as his wife, despite the unusual, scandalous circumstances. The birth in a manger. The shepherds and wise men from the East visiting this special child.

How that child, Jesus, grew to be man and more – He was the son of God, sent to Earth to teach the gospel of peace, and to give His life as an eternal ransom for all humanity, the only means of reconciling sinful men and women to their Creator.

In conclusion to her story, she told of God's unfailing love and explained that His arms were open to embrace each of them, regardless of their pasts.

The women talked amongst one another for quite sometime. As they slowly left the common area, Emma was approached by Teeka.

"Wawa, why did you share your pizza with me?" she asked.

"Because you are my sister," Emma answered.

"But I've been so mean to you . . . ." Teeka replied, obviously moved to conviction.

"Well, that doesn't mean I shouldn't love you," Emma replied.

"Wawa, people don't do that in here. What makes you so different?"

Emma's answer was one word, one name. *"Jesus."*

Troubled, Teeka shook her head. *"Wawa, I heard what you said tonight. But Jesus could never accept me after the things that I've done."*

"You're wrong," Emma kindly insisted. *"All it takes is a willing heart."*

"Well . . . for what it's worth, Wawa, I'm sorry," Teeka finally said.

"Thank you," Emma said. *"I forgive you."*

By the time the call for lights-out came, Teeka was gone, mysteriously transferred without explanation. All of her things vanished as if she had never existed.

Christmas Day came, and Emma spent most of it on the phone with her family.

"Merry Christmas, Eleazar," Emma told her now 12-year-old son, stifling the sobs rising in her throat as she heard him answer, *"Merry Christmas, Mommy. . . . hey, guess what I got today? TWO video games! I thought I would only get one!"*

Her young son couldn't comprehend how miserable his mother really was. She was just away, in a "nice" jail somewhere. Hopefully, he does think it's like the Holiday Inn, Emma thought, recalling Victorien's story of what he had told the children earlier about her new accommodations.

Let him have that gift of innocence, Emma told herself. She then let Eleazar go, realizing he was anxious to try out his gifts.

Deborah, her youngest, was next to take the phone. *"Merry Christmas, Mom. I miss you so much! It's weird without you here. I wish you were home with us."*

Emma's throat grew tighter and a fresh flush of tears spilled out before replying. *"Me, too, Sweetie. I wish I could be there, too . . . so, what did you get today?"*

"*Some gift cards, clothes, and my own phone,*" she said proudly.

Emma, knowing time was running out on the call, again gave her love to her children and waited for Victorien to take the phone.

"*It's hardly Christmas without you,*" he whispered quietly.

More tears. "*Yes,*" Emma replied softly, the disappointment in her voice was unmistakable. "*I would have given anything to celebrate with you today.*"

"*Let's never spend another Christmas apart,*" Victorien said, then added with conviction in his voice, "*We will celebrate soon, when you come home, and I promise that we will make up for all of the celebrations that we have missed!*"

As the two exchanged their love through words, the call was abruptly cut off. "*Your time has expired. If you wish to make a call. . .,"* a mechanical voice declared.

Emma sighed, shaking her head, and returned the handset to its cradle. *You and me, Lord. It's just You and me,* she thought.

Chapter Nine

A Celebration of Faith, the Promise of Freedom

With long life will I satisfy him and show him my salvation. Psalm 91 has special meaning to the Wawa family. They cling to it in desperate times and rely heavily on its stated promise.

The new year had come, and the next ninety days passed at a grinding pace. The Bible studies continued, and Emma would meet, console and pray with many new inmates. The women would come and go frequently, Emily had since been released, and Miranda had been transferred to another facility.

Once again Emma was shuttled to Chicago in the middle of the night. As before, Emma's name had *disappeared* from the processing list. Emma would explain to all of the angry officials, jail personell and inmates that these miracles were just God's way of protecting her.

In early March, Emma was once more in the jail visitation area, talking with Pastor Clark. His encouraging words and prayers of strength and courage always lifted her spirits, and this time the conversation was no different.

"Emma," he grinned, looking her directly in the eyes, *"This is the last time I'm going to visit you in prison. The next time we see each other, you will be a free woman."*

Emma was at peace with this prophetic statement and hopeful.

During that final visit with her pastor, Emma spoke of a letter she had received, signed from eight women, thanking her for leading them to Christ.

"Several months ago I met a girl named Goldie who was here for only one night. She faced a tough sentence, but we prayed that the judge would be kind to

her. The next morning she was gone, and I figured that I'd never hear from her again," Emma smiled.

"The judge not only reduced her sentence, he let her join a Teen Challenge program – just as we had prayed! She's been sharing Jesus with the women in her prison," Emma recounted. "She wrote to tell me that because of the kindness I showed to her, many women have found Jesus."

"God always has a plan," the pastor commented. "It's time for you to have a going-away party because you're not going to be here much longer."

A few days later, Emma came into the common room with armloads of pizza. Soon all the inmates were crowding the tables, eating their fill.

Emma stood and explained that this was her going-away party.

"Six months. My Lord has had me here six months!" she said. "I cherish each relationship that I have made. My 'best friend' has been with me from the beginning, He's with me right now, and He'll always be with me wherever I go."

Suddenly, the room's TV, which had been turned down, roared up to full volume. The guard, was trying his best to drown out what he sensed was too close to a sermon beginning. When the inmates yelled at him to turn it down, he walked away. Frustrated, they gathered closer to Emma, straining to hear her as she continued.

"The most valuable thing that I have learned is to trust only in Jesus and what He says," she told them. *"It is life to hear the voice of the Lord, and it there is nothing better. . ."*

Now, the guard returned, frustrated, and ordered Emma into his office over the protests of the other women. The pizza was one thing, he told her, but all this *preachin'* was a whole different thing. *"Wrap it up,"* he demanded, then let her go.

"Living your life as a daughter of heaven is serious business," Emma resumed with the women, undaunted. *"You must give each day to Him and. . ."*

She had hardly gotten those words out before the guard, angrier now, called her back into the office again.

"What the h*** are you doing? I just told you to stop, and you're still preaching out there!" he shouted at her, and then abruptly dismissed her again.

"Thank you for listening, ladies," Emma concluded when she came back. *"Remember what we talked about. And make sure all that pizza is gone!"*

The next morning Emma heard the official news from a jubilant Victorien that she was finally going home. Her second 90-day sentence was nearing completion.

"The lawyer told me just twenty minutes ago that it's over and you're coming home. It's really over, Sweetie, finally!" he said excitedly.

Several hours later Emma was called into the office. This time it was not by the prison chief who had seemed to so delight in her difficulties. Sitting across the table was a different jail officer, a stranger.

"Well, Ms. Wawa, today is your scheduled release day, but we have a problem," he began.

"What problem?" Emma interrupted.

"The chief was supposed to sign your papers before he left today, and . . . well, I guess he 'forgot' to sign them. You're going to have to wait until he gets back. He's on vacation - until next week." The officer said, a mix of embarrassment and aggravation on his face.

Emma's mind screamed, *enough is enough.* She had not come *this* far only to be delayed in the release God had ordained!

"Next week? No. I'm getting out of here TODAY," Emma firmly declared. *"Immigration said I was to be released TODAY. It's not my fault the chief 'forgot' to sign!"*

This new jail officer obviously didn't like the situation any better than Emma. While insisting there was little he could do to speed her release, he eventually agreed to at least let Emma call Victorien about the snag.

"Victorien, the chief did this on purpose - I know it. While he's on 'vacation,' I'm in prison. He must really hate me!" she cried.

Victorien tried to calm her. There was no gentle way to convince her that waiting another week was going to be easy. Emma heard the signal for an incoming call on Victorien's cell phone. The caller I.D. readout told him it was their lawyer. Emma told him to take it, that somehow she would find a way to call him back.

She hung up and was taken to a holding cell, clueless as to what was transpiring.

Two days later, Emma found herself on a bus, once more headed for Immigration processing in Chicago. Once there, she was taken into a waiting room and greeted by the familiar, unfriendly face of the well-dressed Immigration officer.

"So, you're finally on my list, eh? I've been waiting to deport your a**," he said.

"No. Today I am being RELEASED," she answered.

"Released?" he hurriedly looked at her file and the smirk that had begun to form dropped off his face. "I do not believe this! NO ONE comes HERE to get released!"

"I told you that I would not be deported," Emma reminded him, triumphantly. *"You laughed and mocked me, along with many others, but today, it is YOU that gets to release me."*

More subdued and still shocked, the officer rose, telling her to wait while he processed her papers. As he was leaving, he inquired with a note of apology, *"Uh, is there someone coming to get you?"*

"Yes, my husband, my pastor, and his wife," Emma replied.

A few moments later, the officer returned with the official papers. But he still was trying to wrap his bureaucratic mind around what had happened – or more to the point, what had *not* happened.

"This whole mess makes absolutely no sense," he said, shaking his head in disbelief. He then looked at her, amazed at her calm demeanor.

"Aren't you angry about this?" he asked, genuinely interested in her answer.

"Angry? At who?" she replied.

He remembered Emma well and her insistence that God was in control of her fate and not him. *"Well, angry . . . at God, I guess?"* he suggested.

"He's the one who wanted me here," she told him.

"And you're OK with that?"

Her answer was a firm, confident gaze with a nod.

He shook his head and sighed, *"It's a good Good Friday for you today, Emma. You MUST have a friend up there because no one ever gets processed on holidays."*

Miraculously, as if rescued from a desolate mountain, Emma was released by the well-dressed officer. No apologies or explanations came on that day, just an escort to the exit.

Back in the nursing uniform she was originally arrested in, she stepped through one final set of doors. She saw Victorien and tears followed. She melted into a long embrace with her husband. Without words, a warm, loving and reassuring sense filled them both. Emma sighed deeply. After 183 days in prison, *Emma was finally free!*

Chapter Ten

An Uncertain Future

Emma's return that Good Friday, April 6, 2007, sparked what seemed like an endless celebration. Being reunited with her children brought tears of relief and long embraces. Sephora never left her mother's side; Eleazar amazed her with his newly acquired domestic skills; Deborah had never appeared so grown up. Victorien was overjoyed that his family was together at last.

People came by the house for days on end to rejoice with the Wawas, and some would even spend the night, uninvited but certainly welcomed. The food was limitless, the smiles were vibrant, and the conversations non-stop.

Emma had been home only two weeks when Victorien told her that he had been experiencing an ache in his side. He insisted that it was nothing to be concerned about. In fact, he had gone to the doctor for an exam about a month ago while she was still in prison. Since he had received no news that anything was awry, he didn't give it a second thought.

So the family went about their routines. On Sundays, Emma would get dressed for church in an outfit Victorien picked out for her the night before. The children would smile and giggle as Victorien would boast of his style choices and glamourous sense of fashion.

Emma sat in the front row and watched Victorien as he delivered his message. With her children on either side of her, she proudly smiled.

The points Victorien was making during his sermon seemed to carry more of a personal weight than the simple illustrations he usually drew from scripture.

"As a believer, you do not fear bad news," he said. *"There is no 'bad news' for the believer. We don't need to fear the trials and challenges life brings us. No,*

we must welcome them, because when we get through them, we are stronger in God!"

Emma joined in affirming those words, along with others who nodded *"amens"* in the congregation. But inside her, a nagging question loomed: *Was he preaching about the trials they faced as a family while Emma was imprisoned, or was there something more?*

Later when they arrived home, they checked their messages on the answering machine. Victorien had received a message from his doctor, *"Victorien, call me right away. I have some lab results that we need to discuss. I'm available first thing tomorrow morning, and I really need to speak with you. It's urgent."*

The following morning, Victorien gathered with church officials for their weekly pastoral meeting. One of them received a word of knowledge from the Lord: *"Before we get started, I feel like there is someone here with something important to say."*

Victorien gulped in surprise and then surrendered to what seemed obvious. The Lord wanted him to share about the doctor's message that he'd received.

"The doctor sounded serious and wants me to call him this morning. I think it's about something they found from my blood test," he told them.

As the staff sat together, processing the news, they prayed for a miracle and encouraged Victorien to call his doctor and follow up with him, which he did upon returning home.

His confident façade soon crumbled when the doctor told him what the tests had indicated, but the doctor said that more tests were needed to confirm the findings.

Victorien, shaken by the uncertainty of the situation, waited for the right time to tell Emma that further tests were needed. With the constant presence of visitors in their home, Victorien and Emma seldom had a chance to be together, just the two of them, for longer than a few moments. When the day for additional testing came, Victorien told Emma he would only be at the doctor's office for only a short time, and soon they would have more information.

Victorien's follow-up appointment was supposed to take an hour but ended up taking all day. Emma repeatedly tried calling his cell phone with no answer. Alone in the waiting room, Victorien sat as minutes turned to hours. Then the worst possible news: he was diagnosed with an aggressive form of liver cancer and only four months to live.

This death sentence sent a jolt of shock through Victorien's entire body. A feeling of numbness and disbelief flooded his mind.

It was late in the afternoon when Emma heard the front door close. She saw Victorien and knew something wasn't right, standing in the kitchen, looking into his eyes. Even before he spoke, she could feel her heart sink. Tears formed in her eyes.

"God is good," Victorien whispered. *"They say I have only four months to live, and there is nothing they can do."* Emma had not even been home for a month.

Emma fell to her knees by the kitchen counter. Victorien knelt down, tenderly embracing her and said, *"God is in control. Don't cry; we have so much to be grateful for. I'm here, and we're going to continue serving the Lord."*

Later, alone in prayer, Emma sobbed her heart out to God. Her fists clenched as she alternately rebuked the cancer and pleaded for divine healing. She also prayed for answers to the maelstrom of questions roiling inside her.

"What is this?" she demanded. *"You brought me home for THIS? You should have left me in prison! I can't believe this is happening. This is not You; it cannot be You!"*

No clear answers came. The initial reaction from the Wawa children and the French Church congregation was shock, followed by firm declarations of healing to come. After all, the Lord had delivered Emma from prison and deportation; surely this diagnosis of cancer was just setting the stage for another miracle.

The people of the church prayed in shifts, constantly maintaining a stream of petitions to heaven for Victorien's healing. There were frequent visits to the Wawa home to encourage the ailing pastor's shrinking body and constant offers to help Emma with household duties.

Others stopped by with checks and envelopes of money to help with medical expenses, groceries, and other necessities.

Despite his rapid weight loss in the coming weeks, as the disease took a stronger grip of his body, he did what he had done so often before when facing spiritual crossroads; he went on a fast for several days.

Victorien came out of the fasting period at peace, deciding on a regimen of herbal and natural juice treatments rather than experimental medicines and chemotherapy. His doctors had acknowledged that the latter would do him little good anyway.

Another round of tests several weeks later showed the cancer was growing even more rapidly than expected. Still, he refused to accept what seemed so apparent to others – that he was losing his battle against a savage, merciless disease.

Even as his bright eyes began to turn a dull yellow, his clothes sagged, and his energy diminished to the point where a wheelchair replaced his once strong legs, his faith did not waver.

"In the Bible it says the dry bones will have life," he grimaced one night. *"I'm going to believe, no matter what the doctors say."*

As Emma heard him praying these words, knowing the pain had robbed him of another night's sleep, she lowered her head and began to weep silently. Victorien continued to pray, unaware that his wife was listening.

"Lord Jesus, you know what suffering is. I cannot compare my suffering to your suffering . . . but please, take away this pain! It is robbing me of everything," Victorien gasped.

Emma closed her eyes, lifting her tear-streaked face toward the ceiling. *"Please, Father. Hear him. Let him sleep."*

Her prayer was answered. Victorien was finally able to sleep. The pain relented during the coming nights enough for him to slip into deeper sleep than the days before. Victorien seemed to rally some, at least for a while.

It was only an interlude. Several days later Emma found him in the bathroom, crying as he looked at his skeletal face in the mirror. She rushed to his side and held him in her arms, trying to comfort her husband and encourage him to fight on.

"I am so tired," he whimpered, nodding toward the mirror. *"Look at me! It's terrible."*

"Don't look at that!" Emma said, gently turning his face away from the gaunt reflection.

He let out a ragged sigh. *"Emma, I can't do anything for myself anymore. I can't even pull on my own socks."*

"That's OK. That's why I'm here," Emma answered. *"I love you, Victorien. Don't give up."*

It was a conversation repeated often, in varying forms, over the ensuing weeks. Each time, Emma urged him to hold firm, and each time Victorien would fight back, staving off his exhaustion.

One day, Victorien gently confronted her. *"You've been crying, Emma,"* he said.

"No, I haven't," she lied.

"Yes, you have," he replied with a calm tone. *"Emma, I'm going to be fine,"* he added and then prayed aloud, *"Lord, we belong to you. Even in death, we belong to you."*

Emma shook her head, resolutely, quite upset with his word choice and got up from the couch. *No. Oh, no! I do not accept THAT. Lord, you are going to bring him back from this. You did not send me home from prison and return me to my family . . . for this!* she thought.

Victorien went outside, aware that he had made his wife uncomfortable with his prayer.

Soon thereafter, Sephora came to her, a worry clouding her usually happy face. She had also been in constant prayer with the family, believing that God would miraculously restore their father's health.

"Mom, look at Dad," she said, pointing outside to where her father was sitting in the sun, the warm rays a temporary reprieve from pain and fatigue. *"He looks so . . . sad. That's not my Dad. That's not him!"*

Emma nodded at the sight, and then nudged Sephora toward the door. *"Go sit with him, honey. Just talk with him."*

As they talked Emma thought, *Lord, I'm watching my husband disappear before my eyes.* Emma thought as she listened.

Chapter Eleven

An Exit and an Exhortation

Whether he spoke in French or English, Pastor Wawa's tenor voice seemed to leap from his compact, muscular frame. His exuberance was contagious, a river of melodic, west African-accented words that invited his congregation to a feast of faith.

Victorien's message was recorded as he preached that Sunday in mid-August. The title, *"Dwelling in Christ,"* could have hardly been forgotten by those who heard it. In the months that would follow, as his health rapidly failed, this sermon would become a touchstone for those who loved him – and a bittersweet but precious reminder of his devotion to God, regardless of the circumstances.

"Every man, woman and child eventually must make the same decision," Victorien cautioned. *"Why don't we stay at that higher level, in the house and presence of the Lord? Why would we rather choose to go down to a place where there is danger for us?"* he asked.

Carefully, point by point, he cautioned his listeners about some modern-day detours. A loss of interest in the Word of God is one warning sign. A slackening prayer life is another, and diminishing involvement in gatherings with other believers can quickly follow, Victorien warned.

"It is important for the children of God to come together in unity," he said. *"When even two or three come together, the spirit of the Lord is in our midst. . . . but many people believe the lie that they don't need a relationship with other believers."*

Jesus told of a man who was beaten, robbed and left for dead by bandits on the road. Eventually, like the man in the parable, they find themselves out of their "Jerusalem," walking out of God's presence and becoming easy prey. Victorien said the same threat in the spiritual realm lurks on the paths God's errant children so often take; they turn away from Him and stride toward the downward slope leading to the world's attractions.

"Every time a child of God leaves His presence, the devil is waiting for him like a hungry lion. But when you are in the presence of God, you are secure, whatever may come," Victorien said. "Nothing can come against you! Nothing. When we are in Christ Jesus, we are more than conquerors!"

A weak and strained Victorien looked over the sea of faces before him; they were yet unaware of his cancer diagnosis.

"Jesus, through his sacrifice on the cross, has done the same for us," Victorien reminded the church. Furthermore, "Christ lives in those who believe, giving them the confidence and power to resist darkness and dwell in the presence of the Father, forever."

"I don't know your problems this morning, or what you are facing," he said. "But I do know this one thing: The Good Samaritan is in the house."

After church that day, Emma looked at the gaunt figure of her husband, the pastiness that clouded the drooping skin on his face, and the dullness that frequently invaded his once dancing eyes. She heard the hint of a rattle in his breathing, now becoming more and more labored.

This is taking a lot less time than four months, she thought, quickly rebuking the growing fear that accompanied her realization. *It's hardly been a month! Lord, are you going to take my husband, despite all the prayers going up to you? Look at his faithfulness to You, even now while he suffers. The children need him. . . I need him.*

At home, Victorien would moan softly. *Such pain,* Emma thought. She was tired, down to her bones, from lack of sleep. Even when Victorien was able to slip into a momentary slumber, Emma would wake frequently and stare at her husband. *Is he still breathing? Is he all right?*

Once, Victorien woke with a startle. Emma rushed to his side. *"Emma, the Lord spoke to me,"* he rasped, a look of wonder dawning on his face. *"Not a dream, but a voice, really speaking to me. The Lord said, 'When you fall, I will be there to help you rise up.'"*

Nights came when Victorien would quietly leave the room without Emma knowing. In a panic, she would leap to her feet and begin searching for him. Sometimes, she would find him in the children's doorways, just watching them sleep. Other times, she found him curled up on the living room couch, a sacrifice, allowing his wife an hour or two of slumber, uninterrupted by his agonized groaning and twisting.

Victorien made sacrifices for the children as well. Having been too sick to see his son Eleazar's first junior high football game, he was determined to see the second. Being pushed in a wheelchair, Victorien arrived on the sidelines – and drew the inevitable stares.

"What's wrong with your dad?" the other boys asked. *"He's got cancer,"* Eleazar answered, and on hearing himself say those words, his heart sank with their impact. With family and friends, he had been praying for a miracle, but the significance of his ailing father's arrival was inescapable; time was precious, and there might not be another game.

As the game came to an end, Eleazar noticed that his father had left; pain and fatigue had finally won out.

But Victorien had seen his son play football; he kept the promise he had made, despite the suffering it cost.

A few days after the game, Victorien made it very clear that he wanted to have private conversations with each of the children. Now, alone with his son, he talked to the boy as he would to a man.

"Eleazar, if I . . . if I leave, then you have to make sure that your sisters are treated with honor and respect. You must take care of your mother and make sure she isn't alone," Victorien said.

Victorien looked at his son for a moment and continued: *"You are going to become a strong man of God. In the beginning, you will struggle with a lot of things, but I know you can make it through! Some day, you will find a woman who deserves you as much as you deserve her. Be blessed in all you do, and never lose faith."*

Victorien also called Sephora aside. She treasured her dad's sense of humor, the sight of him laughing at cartoon shows on TV or teasing her – even when he got sick – about her housekeeping stills. Now, there was none of that; she knew this was serious.

"Sephora, you're the oldest. You need to be the bigger person when it comes to forgiveness and making something right. Help your mother, especially in the beginning, and take care of your brother and sister. Always stay with God, read your Bible and pray. Next to those things, the number one thing is your education," Victorien stressed.

Sephora nodded. She had recently gotten a "C" in one of her classes, and her father, who never relented from pushing his children to seek academic excellence, had been disappointed. Sephora had gotten the message and promised to buckle down.

Deborah, the youngest, was a "daddy's girl." Sometimes Victorien would try and help her get ready for church or school by braiding her hair, much to Deborah's dismay. Dad's sense of style was decidedly lacking, she had determined. Victorien would smile, put his hands up in surrender and laugh, *"OK, OK. Fine, then fix it yourself!"*

But now, there was sadness in his eyes as he gently, carefully chose his words. He encouraged her to be strong and steady in her faith, to pray, and to study scripture.

"Deborah, you are the youngest. You need to respect your mother, brother and sister. Get a good education and work hard. Some day, you will meet a man who really loves God - and you," he told her.

On the morning of October 1, 2007, Emma joined her children as they prayed with Victorien, a practice that had become routine ever since his diagnosis. The children finished getting ready and went off to school. As usual Sephora, Eleazar and Deborah did their best to pay attention to their lessons, but their father was always on the forefront of their minds.

That afternoon when the kids got off the bus and walked toward their home, they were alarmed to see fire department paramedics packing up their gear and getting ready to leave.

Mom and Dad were gone. Family members told the children they had been rushed to the hospital in an ambulance just minutes before.

Inside the house, fresh blood covered the floor; it had been Victorien's unrelenting, ragged spell of wracking coughs that had prompted the call to 911.

Still in shock, the children were taken by their aunts and uncles to the hospital and rushed into Victorien's room. There, they saw their mother sobbing and their father, though still conscious, with IVs in his arms and an oxygen feed strapped to his face. His chest was heaving with each breath, the struggle for life starkly apparent.

It had barely been six weeks since the Wawas received the news that Victorien had terminal liver cancer. Now, doctors told Emma, Victorien had perhaps a few hours to live.

The prayers offered inside the room were constant, punctuated with cries of anguish that gave way to the quieter crying and sniffing of reluctant acceptance. Pastor Clark was there too, with his own family, offering comfort. He tenderly told the children that their time with Victorien was short.

"If you have anything you want to tell your father, this will be your final opportunity," the pastor said, his own eyes brimming with tears.

The children approached, but there was little more to say than *"I love you, Dad."* Victorien, too, sensed his heart was beating toward conclusion. In barely audible whispers, he looked at each of them, gathered around his bed, and repeated words that he carefully mouthed when his voiced failed him: *"I love you. I love you. I love . . . ."*

Emma leaned close to Victorien's ear. *"If you are really ready and God wants to take you, I'll let you go,"* she cried.

Victorien looked past his loved ones, with growing delight rippling across his face. He made a failing effort to rise and feebly pointed toward some scene only his eyes could see. *Look!* His expression seemed to say, and then he sagged, his mouth open as his final breath was drawn and released.

A nurse quietly maneuvered around the family to Victorien's side and went through the motions of checking for remaining vital signs. No breathing. No heartbeat. Pupils non-reactive. She looked up, pity in her eyes.

"I'm sorry. He's passed," she said. He was 39 years old.

Emma surrendered to the tidal wave of loss and grief. *"Victorien! Victorien! Victorien!"* she repeatedly cried, at first pushing away those who wished to comfort her, then falling into their compassionate arms.

Sephora, who had held her father's hand to the last, moved into Eleazar's arms, not the strong, "oldest" sister for the moment, but a wounded sister given permission by her younger brother to weep.

"It's OK," Eleazar told her, trying to hold back his own emotions and be "the man" of the family. *"You can cry,"* he said, holding his sister tight. *"You can do whatever you want. It's OK. He's with Jesus now."*

The room emptied, except for Eleazar. He felt stillness in the room as he saw his father's body lying in the bed. There was no pain for him anymore. Inside Eleazar's gut, there was a ragged, raw throbbing, stronger as the shock of his father's death faded.

I can't believe it is really over, he thought. *I'll miss you Dad.*

Chapter Twelve

'Betterness' -- not Bitterness

Victorien Wawa died on October 1, 2007, exactly one year to the day from the launch of the French church he started while Emma was in prison. Instead of a celebration to mark the anniversary, the family was planning a funeral.

Three days after his death, nearly 400 mourners packed the seats and aisles of the church the Wawas called home. Many of those who came that day had flown in from Europe and Africa to honor the man who had been their pastor, counselor, teacher and friend.

Pastor Clark presided over the service. At one point, a recording from Victorien's *Dwelling in Christ* sermon in August was played, letting Victorien, in effect, *preach* his own funeral. It was a cherished moment where many got to hear their beloved brother exhort them, once again, to maintain an unwavering walk of faith and trust in their God.

At the conclusion of the service, people were invited to follow the casket to a nearby cemetery. It was a bright, sunny day, a gentle breeze blowing through the trees, leaves just beginning to turn toward rich autumnal colors. As Emma and her children sat next to the burial site, the comforting crowd gathered behind them.

Pastor Clark opened his Bible and lifted his voice so all could hear as he read I Corinthians 15: *"Listen, I tell you a mystery. We will not all sleep, but we will all be changed — in a flash, in the twinkling of an eye, at the last trumpet. For the trumpet will sound, the dead will be raised imperishable, and we will be changed. For the perishable must clothe itself with the imperishable, and the mortal with immortality."*

Turning to the Gospel of John, he then read Chapter 14: 1-3, offering Jesus' own promises of eternal life for those who love him. *"Do not let your hearts be troubled. Trust in God; trust also in me. In my Father's house are many rooms; if it were not so, I would have told you. I am going there to prepare a place for you. And if I go and prepare a place for you, I will come back and take you to be with me, that you also may be where I am."*

Finally, one by one, the somber crowd filed past the grave, placing flowers on the casket. One blossom became two, then ten, then twenty. When the last of the mourners had gone by, a mound of petals covered Victorien's remains. The fragrance of the flowers punctuated the end of this godly man's life and the end of 15 years of marriage.

Little did Emma know that the days that God had ordained for her to spend in prison were preparing her to deal with the loss of her husband. This tragedy had the potential to sever her relationship with the Lord even more than her prison experience did. In both instances, the choice was hers: to blame God for ruining her life and reject Him, or to trust His unfailing love and accept that His Word is true, regardless of the circumstances.

In the days and weeks that followed, after all the visitors were gone, Emma had time to reflect on the blessing and the loss.

Emma noticed how her children had grown: her first-born, Sephora, 15, older in so many ways, serious about her role as "big sister" and her mother's helpmate; Eleazar, now a strapping 14-year-old; Deborah, her youngest, 12, blossoming into a young woman.

Her children brought a sense of reassurance that seemed to ease the pain of losing Victorien. She could see their father in each one of them. In Sephora, she saw Victorien's leadership. In Eleazar, she saw Victorien's confidence. In Deborah, she saw Victorien's tenderness.

These moments are a down-payment on what will someday come, when my husband will again embrace me and our children, Emma thought to herself.

Not long after the funeral, the four of them gathered in the kitchen to prepare a meal together.

As they sat down to eat, there was a moment of silence. All of them were staring at Victorien's empty seat. After several minutes, without movement or noise, Emma burst into tears. One by one each of them began to cry. They sat there together for several hours and held one another as they recounted their favorite memories as a family. The Lord was healing their broken hearts.

More than 3 years after Victorien went to be with Jesus, Emma sheds tears anew as she remembers Victorien; loneliness remains an almost constant companion. But she has embraced it – along with the certainty of an eventual reunion with the love of her life. Most importantly, there is no bitterness toward God or the law enforcement personnel for keeping her from her husband for more than half of his last year of life.

She has peace with God, choosing to trust rather than question. Emma can both acknowledge the unfairness of it all and even smile about how God has used her trials as an opportunity to share His love with the world.

"After the funeral, so many people stopped by the house. Too many people. Then after that, they

stopped. I understood; people had to get back to their own lives, and now it was time that we got on with ours," Emma recalls.

"The hardest part was in the morning when the kids all went to school. I'd find myself thinking, 'Wow – where is he?' I'd even find myself looking for him. I would end up sitting on the couch in the living room and looking through the window into the back yard, remembering how so often he would be back there, fixing something. Or maybe he'd been at the library, studying, and I would wait for the garage door to open and him to walk in. We are always going to miss him. Yes, he is really gone – but God knows!"

The Wawa family has found strength in their shared faith and in each other.

"The kids shared my bedroom. We had to; I wanted them close to me. That's the way it was for two weeks. Then one night, Eleazar decided to go back to his own room, and I said, 'OK.' The girls did, too, and I had to get used to being alone at night."

Emma reflects on a phone conversation that marks a milestone in the healing that the Lord has brought to her heart.

"One day, a sister in Christ called me from Africa. She said, 'Emma, I'm sorry for what happened to you. You probably don't even remember me, but we met once ten years ago. The Lord is telling me that 'You have too many questions - what happened, what did I do to deserve this, why me. . . . Sister, the Lord wants you to stop questioning and know that He loves you SO MUCH!'"

Emma just listened. *Who are YOU, to say this to ME?* She thought at first, but deep inside she knew the words were true. After she hung up, Emma fell to her knees in prayer.

"Lord, I miss him so much!" she cried.

"Do you trust Me?" was the question always entering her mind. Emma answered, *"Yes, I trust You."*

The gentle voice inside her would repeatedly ask, *"Why can't you believe I am the same God who opened the prison gates?"*

Emma sobbed, finally, surrendering her grief.

"*I keep crying, but that doesn't mean I don't trust You,*" she prayed. "*I know that you love me. You send people to comfort me, you even make them call all the way from Africa.*"

Then the peace of heaven covered her like warm oil.

With time Emma's prayer and perspectives have changed. Emma knows that the Lord guided her out of her valley of mourning and into a new chapter of life.

"*Do something new in my life, Lord,*" she found herself asking one day. "*Do something new in my life, do something new.*" Emma made it a song, and it became her new daily prayer.

She has poured herself into her daycare business, rediscovering her joy through playing and laughter. Emma has dedicated herself to ministry in the French Church, too, taking her place as the spiritual mother to many women in the congregation.

Some of Victorien's final words to her, knowing his own time was short, were about moving out of his pastoral shadow and finding her own path of leadership in the church. At the time, she had serious doubts about the idea.

"He kept saying, 'You can do it!' Victorien put his whole heart and life into the ministry of loving people and serving God. He finished strong in the Lord, and hearing him say that I could do that also was my big turning point. I want to finish strong, like he did - and I realized that to do that, I had to move forward."

"I have decided to continue obeying the Lord and to trust Him completely. The devil is a loser, and in the end, he will cry!"

"I know that God will complete His work in my life and in my family," she says. *"The call from God on me was to no longer to hide in Victorien's shadow. It was now God's time for me to rise up and do what He called me to do."*

"He has given me MORE strength and confidence than ever before to release His kingdom, power, and miraculous love," Emma declares.

"I feel the Lord in everything I do and want to share it with everyone I meet. I have fallen desperately in love with God and will serve Him always," she adds.

Six months of wrongful imprisonment and mistreatment by a faceless system, followed by the sudden, tragic loss of her beloved husband, could have driven Emma to turn from her family and her faith. But instead the crucible of pain has become a vessel of triumph.

Emma declares with mighty wisdom and resolve: *"I choose to see God in everything and realize that I must let my bitterness become betterness. I make that decision every day."*

Clutching her Bible, Emma reads to the congregation gathered before her the well-worn passage from Psalm 91. These words mean more to her now than ever before.

Psalm 91

He who dwells in the secret place of the Most High shall abide under the shadow of the Almighty. I will say of the LORD, "He is my refuge and my fortress; My God, in Him I will trust."

Surely He shall deliver you from the snare of the fowler and from the perilous pestilence. He shall cover you with His feathers, and under His wings you shall take refuge; His truth shall be your shield and buckler.

You shall not be afraid of the terror by night, nor of the arrow that flies by day, nor of the pestilence that walks in darkness, nor of the destruction that lays waste at noonday.

A thousand may fall at your side, and ten thousand at your right hand; but it shall not come near you. Only with your eyes shall you look, and see the reward of the wicked.

Because you have made the LORD, who is my refuge, even the Most High, your dwelling place, no evil shall befall you, nor shall any plague come near your dwelling; for He shall give His angels charge over you, to keep you in all your ways. In their hands they shall bear you up, lest you dash your foot against a stone. You shall tread upon the lion and the cobra, the young lion and the serpent you shall trample underfoot.

"Because he has set his love upon Me, therefore I will deliver him; I will set him on high, because he has known My name. He shall call upon Me, and I will answer him; I will be with him in trouble; I will deliver him and honor him. With long life I will satisfy him, and show him My salvation." (NKJV)

Contact Information & Resources

The True Story of Emma Wawa Continues at:

www.emmawawa.com

Johnny Clark

Johnny.j2c@gmail.com

www.johnnyandnicole.net

(608) 217-4271